My First Story of
CHRISTMAS

Tim Dowley
Illustrated by Roger Langton

CANDLE
BOOKS

Published by Candle Books
an imprint of
Lion Hudson plc
Wilkinson House, Jordan Hill Road,
Oxford OX2 8DR, England
www.lionhudson.com/candle

ISBN 978 1 78128 105 5
e-ISBN 978 1 78128 154 3

First edition 2004
This edition 2014

A catalogue record for this book is available
from the British Library

Printed and bound in China, May 2014, LH17

An Angel Visits Mary

Long ago, in the time of King Herod of Judea,
there lived a girl called Mary.

One day God sent the angel Gabriel to Mary. "Don't be afraid!" he said. "God is pleased with you."

"God is going to give you
a very special baby," said the angel.
"You must call him Jesus!"

Then the angel
disappeared.
But Mary was very happy.
She sang a song to thank God.

Mary loved Joseph, the village carpenter.
Soon they were married.

They began to get ready for the baby.

It was almost time for Mary's baby to be born.

Then the ruler of the country decided
to count all the people.

Mary and Joseph Travel to Bethlehem

So Mary and Joseph went
on a long journey, to a town called
Bethlehem, to be counted.

When at last they arrived in Bethlehem,
Mary was very tired.

Joseph knocked at the door of an inn.

"No room!" said the man.
So they had to sleep in a stable.

Jesus is Born

That night, with the donkey and cows standing close,
Mary's baby boy, Jesus, was born.

In fields nearby,
shepherds were looking after their sheep.

Suddenly an angel appeared. The shepherds were scared. "Don't be afraid!" said the angel.

"Tonight a special baby has been born in Bethlehem. He will save his people."

Then crowds of angels filled the sky, singing,

"Praise God in heaven!"

The angels disappeared as quickly as they had come.
All was dark again.

The shepherds rushed off into Bethlehem.
They had to find the new baby!

The shepherds soon found Mary and Joseph
in the stable – and baby Jesus lying in a manger.

Wise Men Bring Gifts to Jesus

At the time that Jesus was born,
wise men in a far country
were looking at the night sky.

"Look!" said one, "I've never seen that star before."

"It means a new king has been born,"
said a second.

"We must follow the star and find him,"
said the third wise man.

So the wise men set out on a long, hard journey,
following the star by night.

When they arrived in Judea,
they went straight to King Herod's palace.
But the new king was not there.

At last the star stopped over Bethlehem.

As soon as they saw little Jesus,
the wise men knelt down.

They knew he was the new king.
They gave him rich presents:
gold, frankincense, and myrrh.

Each year we remember that first Christmas,
when Jesus was born in a stable.

We give each other presents,
just as the wise men gave presents to Jesus.
And just as God sent Jesus as the best gift of all.